CHRISTIAN HHIKU

The 17-Syllable Devotional

Clark Osborn

A KINGDOM CREATIVE
production
of Aaron & Hur Ministry

http://twitter.com/ChristianHaiku

facebook

www.facebook.com/pages/Christian-Haiku/324198840452

Christian Haiku: The 17-Syllable Devotional
First Edition
Self-Published - © 2010 Clark Osborn

A KINGDOM CREATIVE production
of Aaron & Hur Ministry
www.AaronHur.org - www.ChristianHaiku.com

Layout & Design by
Casey Kashiemer
planetkc3@gmail.com

Unless otherwise noted, Scripture taken from the HOLY BIBLE, NEW INTERNATIONAL VERSION®. Copyright © 1973, 1978, 1984 Biblica. Used by permission of Zondervan. All rights reserved. The "NIV" and "New International Version" trademarks are registered in the United States Patent and Trademark Office by Biblica. Use of either trademark requires the permission of Biblica.

Scripture quotations marked NASB are taken from the NEW AMERICAN STANDARD BIBLE®, Copyright © 1960, 1962, 1963, 1968, 1971, 1972, 1973, 1975, 1977, 1995 by The Lockman Foundation. Used by permission.

Scripture quotations marked MSG taken from The Message.
Copyright © 1993, 1994, 1995, 1996, 2000, 2001, 2002.
Used by permission of NavPress Publishing Group.

Scripture quotations marked NLT are taken from the Holy Bible, New Living Translation, copyright 1996, 2004. Used by permission of Tyndale House Publishers, Inc., Wheaton, Illinois 60189. All rights reserved.

International Standard Book Number: 978-0-615-41508-6

Printed in the USA

Inspiration

Haiku is a Japanese poetry form that consists of just three lines, the first and last containing just five syllables and the middle one seven. Two years ago, I had never even heard of Haiku. Our son Josh brought it home from school as a homework assignment. Once he explained what it was and how it worked, I was hooked. A wordsmith at heart with a penchant for being more than just a tad verbose, Haiku forced me to get my thoughts out in just 17-syllables. While my early efforts were more of a secular and comedic nature, God quickly showed me that this was something He had given me to do for Him. To borrow a line from the movie "Chariots of Fire", I feel God's pleasure when I write.

Of course I'm really not writing anything that hasn't already been written, I'm just writing it a little different. To be certain, it is the Word of God and the Holy Spirit which have provided any and all inspiration in the following pages.

Acknowledgements

Many thanks go to God, my wife Julie, my stepmother Lu, my dad Arthur, my friend Casey and a long list of other family and friends that would take up many pages. Without the investments that each of you have made in my life and this project, this book certainly could never have been written.

Thanks also to the many of you who committed to supporting this project, giving me the confidence and the resources to pursue getting "Christian Haiku" into print.

Dedication

This book is dedicated to Jesus, my wife Julie, my two sons Joshua and Timothy and to the memories of Arthur, Amy, Nancy, Ted & Donna.

Contents (by title)

KNOWING JESUS

Helping out the poor
Taking care of the needy
That's knowing Jesus

He defended the cause of the poor and needy, and so all went well. Is that not what it means to know me?" declares the LORD.

Jeremiah 22:16

"Then the righteous will answer him, 'Lord, when did we see you hungry and feed you, or thirsty and give you something to drink? When did we see you a stranger and invite you in, or needing clothes and clothe you? When did we see you sick or in prison and go to visit you?' "The King will reply, 'I tell you the truth, whatever you did for one of the least of these brothers of mine, you did for me.'

Matthew 25:37-40

"CLANG"

*If you don't have love
Nothing else you do matters
"Clang" goes the cymbal*

If I speak in the tongues of men and of angels, but have not love, I am only a resounding gong or a clanging cymbal. If I have the gift of prophecy and can fathom all mysteries and all knowledge, and if I have a faith that can move mountains, but have not love, I am nothing. If I give all I possess to the poor and surrender my body to the flames, but have not love, I gain nothing.

Love is patient, love is kind. It does not envy, it does not boast, it is not proud. It is not rude, it is not self-seeking, it is not easily angered, it keeps no record of wrongs. Love does not delight in evil but rejoices with the truth. It always protects, always trusts, always hopes, always perseveres. Love never fails.

1 Cor 13:1-8a

DECELERATION

Freneticism
Sucking the life out of life
Deceleration

"Step out of the traffic! Take a long, loving look at me, your High God, above politics, above everything."

Psalm 46:10 (MSG)

"Slow down. Take a deep breath. What's the hurry? Why wear yourself out? Just what are you after anyway?

Jeremiah 2:25 (MSG)

"Are you tired? Worn out? Burned out on religion? Come to me. Get away with me and you'll recover your life. I'll show you how to take a real rest. Walk with me and work with me—watch how I do it. Learn the unforced rhythms of grace. I won't lay anything heavy or ill-fitting on you. Keep company with me and you'll learn to live freely and lightly."

Matthew 11:28-30 (MSG)

COMMODITIES

Going for the gold?
Try setting your sights higher
God commodities

So that the proof of your faith, being more precious than gold which is perishable, even though tested by fire, may be found to result in praise and glory and honor at the revelation of Jesus Christ;

1 Peter 1:7 (NASB)

But Peter said, "I do not possess silver and gold, but what I do have I give to you: In the name of Jesus Christ the Nazarene-- walk!"

Acts 3:6 (NASB)

How much better it is to get wisdom than gold! And to get understanding is to be chosen above silver.

Prov 16:16 (NASB)

FORGIVE

Forgiving yourself
When you don't forgive others
You will find it hard

Then the king called in the man he had forgiven and said, 'You evil servant! I forgave you that tremendous debt because you pleaded with me. Shouldn't you have mercy on your fellow servant, just as I had mercy on you?' Then the angry king sent the man to prison to be tortured until he had paid his entire debt. "That's what my heavenly Father will do to you if you refuse to forgive your brothers and sisters from your heart."

Matthew 18:32-35 (NLT)

Make allowance for each other's faults, and forgive anyone who offends you. Remember, the Lord forgave you, so you must forgive others. Above all, clothe yourselves with love, which binds us all together in perfect harmony.

Col 3:13-14 (NLT)

JESUS IS LORD

Name above all names
Yeshua HaMaschiach
Satan's shibboleth

Your attitude should be the same as that of Christ Jesus: Who, being in very nature God, did not consider equality with God something to be grasped, but made himself nothing, taking the very nature of a servant, being made in human likeness. And being found in appearance as a man, he humbled himself and became obedient to death— even death on a cross! Therefore God exalted him to the highest place and gave him the name that is above every name, that at the name of Jesus every knee should bow, in heaven and on earth and under the earth, and every tongue confess that Jesus Christ is Lord, to the glory of God the Father.

Philippians 2:5-11

TIME

*When it's all over
Our greatest regret may be
How we spent our time*

Teach us to number our days aright, that we may gain a heart of wisdom.

Psalm 90:12

Show me, O LORD, my life's end and the number of my days; let me know how fleeting is my life.

Psalm 39:4

Man is like a breath; his days are like a fleeting shadow.

Psalm 144:4

KINGDOM

So brand me a fool
It is a great compliment
Upside-down Kingdom

Remember, dear brothers and sisters, that few of you were wise
in the world's eyes or powerful or wealthy when God called
you. Instead, God chose things the world considers foolish in
order to shame those who think they are wise. And he chose
things that are powerless to shame those who are powerful.
God chose things despised by the world, things counted as
nothing at all, and used them to bring to nothing what the
world considers important. As a result, no one can ever boast
in the presence of God.

1 Corinthians 1:26-29 (NLT)

"So the last will be first, and the first will be last."

Matthew 20:16

NAVIGATION

Life navigation
If you can't take direction
You're gonna' get lost

I know, God, that mere mortals can't run their own lives, That men and women don't have what it takes to take charge of life. So correct us, God, as you see best. Don't lose your temper. That would be the end of us.

Jeremiah 10:23-24 (MSG)

Show me the right path, O Lord; point out the road for me to follow.

Psalm 25:4 (NLT)

Your teacher will be right there, local and on the job, urging you on whenever you wander left or right: "This is the right road. Walk down this road."

Isaiah 30:21 (MSG)

Train me, God, to walk straight; then I'll follow your true path.

Psalm 86:11a (MSG)

NEW HEART

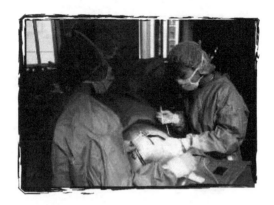

The eyes of my heart
So prone to lust and loathing
I need a transplant

I will give them an undivided heart and put a new spirit in them; I will remove from them their heart of stone and give them a heart of flesh. Then they will follow my decrees and be careful to keep my laws. They will be my people, and I will be their God.

Ezekiel 11:19-20

Create in me a pure heart, O God, and renew a steadfast spirit within me.

Psalm 51:10

I will give them a heart to know me, that I am the LORD. They will be my people, and I will be their God, for they will return to me with all their heart.

Jeremiah 24:7

REWARD

'Tis far more noble
To serve in obscurity
Sans recognition

Beware of practicing your righteousness before men to be noticed by them; otherwise you have no reward with your Father who is in heaven. So when you give to the poor, do not sound a trumpet before you, as the hypocrites do in the synagogues and in the streets, so that they may be honored by men Truly I say to you, they have their reward in full. But when you give to the poor, do not let your left hand know what your right hand is doing, so that your giving will be in secret; and your Father who sees what is done in secret will reward you.

Matthew 6:1-4 (NASB)

Before his downfall a man's heart is proud, but humility comes before honor.

Proverbs 18:12

THE WAY

"No thank you Jesus
I'll find my own way to God"
All attempts futile

Jesus told him, "I am the way, the truth, and the life. No one can come to the Father except through me.

John 14:6 (NLT)

Now all of us can come to the Father through the same Holy Spirit because of what Christ has done for us.

Ephesians 2:18 (NLT)

For Jesus is the one referred to in the Scriptures, where it says 'The stone that you builders rejected has now become the cornerstone.' There is salvation in no one else! God has given no other name under heaven by which we must be saved.

Acts 4:11-12 (NLT)

GET GOING

Inactivity
Leads to cardiology
Equipment failures

Or do you not know that your body is a temple of the Holy Spirit who is in you, whom you have from God, and that you are not your own? For you have been bought with a price: therefore glorify God in your body.

1 Corinthians 6:19-20 (NASB)

Do you not know? Have you not heard? The Everlasting God, the LORD, the Creator of the ends of the earth Does not become weary or tired His understanding is inscrutable. He gives strength to the weary, And to him who lacks might He increases power. Though youths grow weary and tired, And vigorous young men stumble badly, Yet those who wait for the LORD Will gain new strength; They will mount up with wings like eagles, They will run and not get tired, They will walk and not become weary.

Isaiah 40:28-31 (NASB)

HOPE LIVES

Don't EVER give up!
There's light at your tunnel's end
Hope has a heartbeat

Then Jesus told his disciples a parable to show them that they should always pray and not give up.

Luke 18:1

But as for me, I will always have hope; I will praise you more and more.

Psalm 71:14

Let us not become weary in doing good, for at the proper time we will reap a harvest if we do not give up.

Galatians 6:9

Not only so, but we also rejoice in our sufferings, because we know that suffering produces perseverance; perseverance, character; and character, hope. And hope does not disappoint us, because God has poured out his love into our hearts by the Holy Spirit, whom he has given us.

Romans 5:3-5

ENCOURAGEMENT

Kind word, good timing
Sometimes that is all it takes
To make someone's day

Worry weighs us down; a cheerful word picks us up.

Proverbs 12:25 (MSG)

The right word at the right time is like a custom-made piece of jewelry,

Proverbs 25:11 (MSG)

But encourage one another day after day, as long as it is still called "Today," so that none of you will be hardened by the deceitfulness of sin.

Hebrews 3:13 (NASB)

Do not let any unwholesome talk come out of your mouths, but only what is helpful for building others up according to their needs, that it may benefit those who listen.

Ephesians 4:29

WORD POWER

The power of words
Cannot be overstated
When the words are God's

Then God said, "Let there be light"; and there was light.

Genesis 1:3 (NASB)

In the beginning was the Word, and the Word was with God, and the Word was God. He was in the beginning with God. All things came into being through Him, and apart from Him nothing came into being that has come into being.

John 1:1-3 (NASB)

The Son is the radiance of God's glory and the exact representation of his being, sustaining all things by his powerful word.

Hebrews 1:3a

HEAVEN

I'm movin' on up
From muck and mire to mansion
My place by God's grace

He lifted me out of the slimy pit, out of the mud and mire; he set my feet on a rock and gave me a firm place to stand.

Psalm 40:2

In my Father's house are many rooms; if it were not so, I would have told you. I am going there to prepare a place for you. And if I go and prepare a place for you, I will come back and take you to be with me that you also may be where I am.

John 14:2-3

All of us also lived among them at one time, gratifying the cravings of our sinful nature and following its desires and thoughts. Like the rest, we were by nature objects of wrath. But because of his great love for us, God, who is rich in mercy, made us alive with Christ even when we were dead in transgressions—it is by grace you have been saved.

Ephesians 2:3-5

PEACE

For my anxiousness
Prayer is the best sedative
True peace is priceless

Don't fret or worry. Instead of worrying, pray. Let petitions and praises shape your worries into prayers, letting God know your concerns. Before you know it, a sense of God's wholeness, everything coming together for good, will come and settle you down. It's wonderful what happens when Christ displaces worry at the center of your life.

Philippians 4:6-7 (MSG)

You will keep in perfect peace all who trust in you, all whose thoughts are fixed on you!

Isaiah 26:3 (NLT)

I've told you all this so that trusting me, you will be unshakable and assured, deeply at peace. In this godless world you will continue to experience difficulties. But take heart! I've conquered the world.

John 16:33 (MSG)

REJECTION

God is our Father
A hard picture for many
Rejected at home

Even if my father and mother abandon me, the Lord will hold me close.

Psalm 27:10 (NLT)

God is not a man, so he does not lie. He is not human, so he does not change his mind. Has he ever spoken and failed to act? Has he ever promised and not carried it through?

Numbers 23:19 (NLT)

Do not be afraid or discouraged, for the Lord will personally go ahead of you. He will be with you; he will neither fail you nor abandon you.

Deuteronomy 31:6 (NLT)

See how very much our Father loves us, for he calls us his children, and that is what we are!

1 John 3:1 (NLT)

BAGGAGE

*Guilt, shame, fear, worry
Baggage you're not to carry
Check it with Jesus*

Then Jesus said, "Come to me, all of you who are weary and carry heavy burdens, and I will give you rest. Take my yoke upon you. Let me teach you, because I am humble and gentle at heart, and you will find rest for your souls.

Matthew 11:28-29 (NLT)

Give all your worries and cares to God, for he cares about you.

1 Peter 5:7 (NLT)

So now there is no condemnation for those who belong to Christ Jesus.

Romans 8:1 (NLT)

DESTINATION

A foolish gambit
Dice-rolling for destiny
In the end you crap

"But you who abandon me, your God, who forget the holy mountains, Who hold dinners for Lady Luck and throw cocktail parties for Sir Fate, Well, you asked for it. Fate it will be: your destiny, Death. For when I invited you, you ignored me; when I spoke to you, you brushed me off. You did the very things I exposed as evil; you chose what I hate."

Isaiah 65:11-12 (MSG)

And you also were included in Christ when you heard the word of truth, the gospel of your salvation. Having believed, you were marked in him with a seal, the promised Holy Spirit, who is a deposit guaranteeing our inheritance until the redemption of those who are God's possession—to the praise of his glory.

Ephesians 1:13-14

REFLECTION

It's not fair to God
To say He doesn't exist
Due to flawed Christians

I pray also for those who will believe in me through their message, that all of them may be one, Father, just as you are in me and I am in you. May they also be in us so that the world may believe that you have sent me. I have given them the glory that you gave me, that they may be one as we are one: I in them and you in me. May they be brought together to complete unity to let the world know that you sent me and have loved them even as you have loved me.

John 17:20-23

Therefore, as God's chosen people, holy and dearly loved, clothe yourselves with compassion, kindness, humility, gentleness and patience. Bear with each other and forgive whatever grievances you may have against one another. Forgive as the Lord forgave you. And over all these virtues, put on love, which binds them all together in perfect unity.

Colossians 3:12-14

RESURRECTION

Risen from the grave
He holds the keys to death, Hades
Jesus is alive

I am the Living One; I was dead, and behold I am alive for ever and ever! And I hold the keys of death and Hades.

Revelation 1:18

The angel spoke to the women: "There is nothing to fear here. I know you're looking for Jesus, the One they nailed to the cross. He is not here. He was raised, just as he said. Come and look at the place where he was placed. "Now, get on your way quickly and tell his disciples, 'He is risen from the dead. He is going on ahead of you to Galilee. You will see him there.' That's the message.

Matthew 28:5-7 (MSG)

And if the Spirit of him who raised Jesus from the dead is living in you, he who raised Christ from the dead will also give life to your mortal bodies through his Spirit, who lives in you.

Romans 8:11

ATTITUDE

Spent too many years
On Negativity Street
It's time for a move

You were taught, with regard to your former way of life, to put off your old self, which is being corrupted by its deceitful desires; to be made new in the attitude of your minds; and to put on the new self, created to be like God in true righteousness and holiness.

Ephesians 4:22-24

A cheerful disposition is good for your health; gloom and doom leave you bone-tired.

Proverbs 17:22 (MSG)

Don't copy the behavior and customs of this world, but let God transform you into a new person by changing the way you think. Then you will learn to know God's will for you, which is good and pleasing and perfect.

Romans 12:2 (NLT)

ACTION

Annul apathy
Abrogate ambivalence
Culture compassion

So, as those who have been chosen of God, holy and beloved, put on a heart of compassion, kindness, humility, gentleness and patience;

Colossians 3:12 (NASB)

Therefore if there is any encouragement in Christ, if there is any consolation of love, if there is any fellowship of the Spirit, if any affection and compassion, make my joy complete by being of the same mind, maintaining the same love, united in spirit, intent on one purpose. Do nothing from selfishness or empty conceit, but with humility of mind regard one another as more important than yourselves; do not merely look out for your own personal interests, but also for the interests of others.

Phil 2:1-4 (NASB)

HOME

REAL estate market
Looking stronger than ever
Heaven is my home

In My Father's house are many dwelling places; if it were not so,
I would have told you; for I go to prepare a place for you. If I go
and prepare a place for you, I will come again and receive you to
Myself, that where I am, there you may be also.

John 14:2-3 (NASB)

For we know that if the earthly tent which is our house is torn
down, we have a building from God, a house not made with
hands, eternal in the heavens. For indeed in this house we groan,
longing to be clothed with our dwelling from heaven,

1 Corinthians 5:1-2 (NASB)

UNCONDITIONAL

Holy hoop-jumping
Theater of the absurd
We don't earn his love

Answer this question: Does the God who lavishly provides you with his own presence, his Holy Spirit, working things in your lives you could never do for yourselves, does he do these things because of your strenuous moral striving or because you trust him to do them in you? Don't these things happen among you just as they happened with Abraham? He believed God, and that act of belief was turned into a life that was right with God.

Galatians 3:5-6 (MSG)

For by grace you have been saved through faith; and that not of yourselves, it is the gift of God; not as a result of works, so that no one may boast.

Ephesians 2:8-9 (NASB)

RIVER OF LOVE

True love is outsourced
It's flowing down from God's throne
My heart's headwaters

Beloved, let us love one another, for love is from God; and everyone who loves is born of God and knows God.

1 John 4:7 (NASB)

Then he showed me a river of the water of life, clear as crystal,
coming from the throne of God and of the Lamb,

Revelation 22:1 (NASB)

and hope does not disappoint, because the love of God has been
poured out within our hearts through the Holy Spirit who was
given to us.

Romans 5:5 (NASB)

RELEASE

Deliver me God
From what haunts, hurts, holds, hinders
Set me free to run

The Spirit of the Sovereign Lord is upon me, for the Lord has anointed me to bring good news to the poor. He has sent me to comfort the brokenhearted and to proclaim that captives will be released and prisoners will be freed.

Isaiah 61:1 (NLT)

He heals the brokenhearted and bandages their wounds.

Psalm 147:3 (NLT)

No, dear brothers and sisters, I have not achieved it, but I focus on this one thing: Forgetting the past and looking forward to what lies ahead, I press on to reach the end of the race and receive the heavenly prize for which God, through Christ Jesus, is calling us.

Philippians 3:13-14 (NLT)

ON GUARD

Be ever alert
New level brings new devil
No weapon prospers

Keep a cool head. Stay alert. The Devil is poised to pounce, and would like nothing better than to catch you napping. Keep your guard up.

1 Peter 5:8 (MSG)

no weapon forged against you will prevail, and you will refute every tongue that accuses you.

Isaiah 54:17a

Put on the full armor of God so that you can take your stand against the devil's schemes. For our struggle is not against flesh and blood, but against the rulers, against the authorities, against the powers of this dark world and against the spiritual forces of evil in the heavenly realms. Therefore put on the full armor of God, so that when the day of evil comes, you may be able to stand your ground, and after you have done everything, to stand.

Ephesians 6:11-13

SACRIFICE

Fully-yielded will
Gritty determination
Led Christ to the cross

fixing our eyes on Jesus, the author and perfecter of faith, who for the joy set before Him endured the cross, despising the shame, and has sat down at the right hand of the throne of God.

Hebrews 12:2 (NASB)

saying, "Father, if You are willing, remove this cup from Me; yet not My will, but Yours be done."

Luke 22:42 (NASB)

I am the good shepherd, and I know My own and My own know Me, even as the Father knows Me and I know the Father; and I lay down My life for the sheep.

John 10:14-15 (NASB)

and walk in love, just as Christ also loved you and gave Himself up for us, an offering and a sacrifice to God as a fragrant aroma.

Ephesians 5:2 (NASB)

INTEGRITY

Verbal commitments
That don't give birth to action
Are impotent vows

"Tell me what you think of this story: A man had two sons. He went up to the first and said, 'Son, go out for the day and work in the vineyard.' "The son answered, 'I don't want to.' Later on he thought better of it and went. "The father gave the same command to the second son. He answered, 'Sure, glad to.' But he never went. "Which of the two sons did what the father asked?" They said, "The first."

Matthew 21:28-31 (MSG)

Whatever your lips utter you must be sure to do, because you made your vow freely to the LORD your God with your own mouth.

Deuteronomy 23:23

IDENTITY

My significance
Found in this reality:
I'm a child of God

What marvelous love the Father has extended to us! Just look at it—we're called children of God! That's who we really are.

1 John 3:1a (MSG)

You can tell for sure that you are now fully adopted as his own children because God sent the Spirit of his Son into our lives crying out, "Papa! Father!" Doesn't that privilege of intimate conversation with God make it plain that you are not a slave, but a child? And if you are a child, you're also an heir, with complete access to the inheritance.

Galatians 4:6-7 (MSG)

So you have not received a spirit that makes you fearful slaves. Instead, you received God's Spirit when he adopted you as his own children. Now we call him, "Abba, Father." For his Spirit joins with our spirit to affirm that we are God's children.

Romans 8:15-16 (NLT)

REALITY

*Six out of seven
Still won't get you to heaven
Gotta be perfect*

So we are Christ's ambassadors; God is making his appeal through us. We speak for Christ when we plead, "Come back to God!" For God made Christ, who never sinned, to be the offering for our sin, so that we could be made right with God through Christ.

2 Corinthians 5:20-21 (NLT)

So we tell others about Christ, warning everyone and teaching everyone with all the wisdom God has given us. We want to present them to God, perfect in their relationship to Christ.

Colossians 1:28 (NLT)

But because Jesus lives forever, his priesthood lasts forever. Therefore he is able, once and forever, to savethose who come to God through him. He lives forever to intercede with God on their behalf. He is the kind of high priest we need because he is holy and blameless, unstained by sin.

Hebrews 7:24-26 (NLT)

INTIMACY

Quiet time with God
If you're not intentional
It just won't happen

"Be still, and know that I am God!

Psalm 46:10a (NLT)

The LORD is my shepherd, I shall not want. He makes me lie down in green pastures; He leads me beside quiet waters. He restores my soul;

Psalm 23:1-3a (NASB)

As the deer pants for streams of water, so my soul pants for you, O God. My soul thirsts for God, for the living God. When can I go and meet with God?

Psalm 42:1-2

Before daybreak the next morning, Jesus got up and went out to an isolated place to pray.

Mark 1:35 (NLT)

FUEL

Running out of gas?
Get up and go up and went?
Fill 'er up Jesus

God makes his people strong. God gives his people peace.

Psalm 29:11 (MSG)

We pray that you'll have the strength to stick it out over the long haul—not the grim strength of gritting your teeth but the glory-strength God gives. It is strength that endures the unendurable and spills over into joy, thanking the Father who makes us strong enough to take part in everything bright and beautiful that he has for us.

Colossians 1:11-12 (MSG)

For I can do everything through Christ, who gives me strength.

Philippians 4:13 (NLT)

LISTEN

"I have no comment"
Far too infrequently heard
Mouths runneth over

Understand this, my dear brothers and sisters: You must all be quick to listen, slow to speak, and slow to get angry. "

James 1:19 (NLT)

The more talk, the less truth; the wise measure their words.

Proverbs 10:19 (MSG)

Watch your words and hold your tongue; you'll save yourself a lot of grief.

Proverbs 21:23 (MSG)

Peter broke in, "Master, this is a great moment! What would you think if I built three memorials here on the mountain—one for you, one for Moses, one for Elijah?" While he was going on like this, babbling, a light-radiant cloud enveloped them, and sounding from deep in the cloud a voice: "This is my Son, marked by my love, focus of my delight. Listen to him."

Matthew 17:4-5 (MSG)

SCOREKEEPING

God doesn't keep score
So neither should you or I
Mercy triumphant

Lord, if you kept a record of our sins, who, O Lord, could ever survive?

Psalm 130:3 (NLT)

For God was in Christ, reconciling the world to himself, no longer counting people's sins against them. And he gave us this wonderful message of reconciliation.

2 Corinthians 5:19 (NLT)

Love is patient, love is kind. It does not envy, it does not boast, it is not proud. It is not rude, it is not self-seeking, it is not easily angered, it keeps no record of wrongs.

1 Corinthians 13:4-5

because judgment without mercy will be shown to anyone who has not been merciful. Mercy triumphs over judgment!

James 2:3

HUMILITY

Touching the lepers
Hanging with dregs and outcasts
That is my Jesus

Passing along, Jesus saw a man at his work collecting taxes. His name was Matthew. Jesus said, "Come along with me." Matthew stood up and followed him. Later when Jesus was eating supper at Matthew's house with his close followers, a lot of disreputable characters came and joined them. When the Pharisees saw him keeping this kind of company, they had a fit, and lit into Jesus' followers. "What kind of example is this from your Teacher, acting cozy with crooks and riffraff?" Jesus, overhearing, shot back, "Who needs a doctor: the healthy or the sick? Go figure out what this Scripture means: 'I'm after mercy, not religion.' I'm here to invite outsiders, not coddle insiders."

Matthew 9:9-13 (MSG)

EXPECTANCY

Always hope for the best
Everything's redeemable
Only way to live

And we know that God causes everything to work together for
the good of those who love God and are called according to his
purpose for them.

Romans 8:28 (NLT)

Yes, and I will continue to rejoice, for I know that through your
prayers and the help given by the Spirit of Jesus Christ, what
has happened to me will turn out for my deliverance.

Phil 1:19

Joseph replied, "Don't be afraid. Do I act for God? Don't you
see, you planned evil against me but God used those same plans
for my good, as you see all around you right now—life for many
people.

Genesis 50:20 (MSG)

FOCUS

Eyes turn to Jesus
Trouble's flood waters recede
As my focus shifts

Therefore, since we are surrounded by such a great cloud of witnesses, let us throw off everything that hinders and the sin that so easily entangles, and let us run with perseverance the race marked out for us. Let us fix our eyes on Jesus, the author and perfecter of our faith, who for the joy set before him endured the cross, scorning its shame, and sat down at the right hand of the throne of God. Consider him who endured such opposition from sinful men, so that you will not grow weary and lose heart.

Hebrews 12:1-3

"Do not be afraid, for I have ransomed you. I have called you by name; you are mine. When you go through deep waters, I will be with you. When you go through rivers of difficulty, you will not drown. When you walk through the fire of oppression, you will not be burned up; the flames will not consume you."

Isaiah 43:1b-2 (NLT)

SECURITY

Money won't save you
Find security in God
Best retirement plan

The rich think of their wealth as a strong defense; they imagine
it to be a high wall of safety.

> Proverbs 18:11 (NLT)

Don't hoard treasure down here where it gets eaten by moths
and corroded by rust or—worse!—stolen by burglars. Stockpile
treasure in heaven, where it's safe from moth and rust and burglars.

> Matthew 6:19-20 (MSG)

The righteous will see it and be amazed. They will laugh and
say, "Look what happens to mighty warriors who do not trust in
God. They trust their wealth instead and grow more and more
bold in their wickedness." But I am like an olive tree, thriving in
the house of God. I will always trust in God's unfailing love.

> Psalm 52:6-8 (NLT)

PROMOTION

The highest office
Belongs to the Servant King
Humble promotion

You must have the same attitude that Christ Jesus had. Though he was God, he did not think of equality with God as something to cling to. Instead, he gave up his divine privileges; he took the humble position of a slave and was born as a human being. When he appeared in human form, he humbled himself in obedience to God and died a criminal's death on a cross. Therefore, God elevated him to the place of highest honor and gave him the name above all other names, that at the name of Jesus every knee should bow, in heaven and on earth and under the earth, and every tongue confess that Jesus Christ is Lord, to the glory of God the Father.

Philippians 2:5-11 (NLT)

Whoever exalts himself shall be humbled; and whoever humbles himself shall be exalted.

Matthew 23:12 (NASB)

HEALING

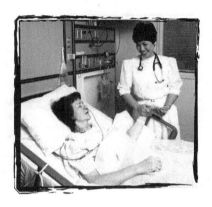

Jehovah Rophe
For malaise and malady
The best prescription

And He said, "If you will give earnest heed to the voice of the LORD your God, and do what is right in His sight, and give ear to His commandments, and keep all His statutes, I will put none of the diseases on you which I have put on the Egyptians; for I, the LORD, am your healer."

Exodus 15:26 (NASB)

But he was pierced for our transgressions, he was crushed for our iniquities; the punishment that brought us peace was upon him, and by his wounds we are healed.

Isaiah 53:5

Heal me, O LORD, and I will be healed; save me and I will be saved, for you are the one I praise.

Jeremiah 17:14

UNDER CONSTRUCTION

A work in progress
I have not yet been transformed
But I'm transforming

And we, who with unveiled faces all reflect the Lord's glory, are being transformed into his likeness with ever-increasing glory, which comes from the Lord, who is the Spirit.

2 Corinthians 3:18

For instance, we know that when these bodies of ours are taken down like tents and folded away, they will be replaced by resurrection bodies in heaven—God-made, not handmade—and we'll never have to relocate our "tents" again. Sometimes we can hardly wait to move— and so we cry out in frustration. Compared to what's coming, living conditions around here seem like a stopover in an unfurnished shack, and we're tired of it! We've been given a glimpse of the real thing, our true home, our resurrection bodies! The Spirit of God whets our appetite by giving us a taste of what's ahead. He puts a little of heaven in our hearts so that we'll never settle for less.

2 Corinthians 5:1-5 (MSG)

CAPTIVITY

So many enslaved
But most are not held captive
Chained by our choices

They promise freedom, but they themselves are slaves of sin and corruption. For you are a slave to whatever controls you.

2 Peter 2:19 (NLT)

The sinful nature wants to do evil, which is just the opposite of what the Spirit wants. And the Spirit gives us desires that are the opposite of what the sinful nature desires. These two forces are constantly fighting each other, so you are not free to carry out your good intentions.

Galatians 5:17 (NLT)

It was for freedom that Christ set us free; therefore keep standing firm and do not be subject again to a yoke of slavery.

Galatians 5:1 (NASB)

PERSPECTIVE

I see my failures
The me I'm going to be
That is who God sees

For I am confident of this very thing, that He who began a good work in you will perfect it until the day of Christ Jesus.

Philippians 1:6 (NASB)

'For I know the plans that I have for you,' declares the LORD, ' plans for welfare and not for calamity to give you a future and a hope.

Jeremiah 29:11 (NASB)

Who is a God like you, who pardons sin and forgives the transgression of the remnant of his inheritance? You do not stay angry forever but delight to show mercy. You will again have compassion on us; you will tread our sins underfoot and hurl all our iniquities into the depths of the sea.

Micah 7:18-19

PERSONAL

Don't be offended
But take it personally
God's word is for you

Then he said: 'The God of our fathers has chosen you to know his will and to see the Righteous One and to hear words from his mouth.

Acts 22:14

God means what he says. What he says goes. His powerful Word is sharp as a surgeon's scalpel, cutting through everything, whether doubt or defense, laying us open to listen and obey. Nothing and no one is impervious to God's Word. We can't get away from it—no matter what.

Hebrews 4:12-13 (MSG)

Jesus provided far more God-revealing signs than are written down in this book. These are written down so you will believe that Jesus is the Messiah, the Son of God, and in the act of believing, have real and eternal life in the way he personally revealed it.

John 20:30-31 (MSG)

APPEARANCES

Outward appearance
Makes no difference to God
He looks at the heart

But God told Samuel, "Looks aren't everything. Don't be impressed with his looks and stature. I've already eliminated him. God judges persons differently than humans do. Men and women look at the face; God looks into the heart."

1 Samuel 16:7 (MSG)

As for those who seemed to be important—whatever they were makes no difference to me; God does not judge by external appearance—those men added nothing to my message.

Galatians 2:6

Even hell holds no secrets from God— do you think he can't read human hearts?

Proverbs 15:11 (MSG)

GENTLE GIANT

Jesus Messiah
The Lamb with a lion's roar
The light of the world

Then I began to weep greatly because no one was found worthy to open the book or to look into it; and one of the elders said to me, "Stop weeping; behold, the Lion that is from the tribe of Judah, the Root of David, has overcome so as to open the book and its seven seals." And I saw between the throne (with the four living creatures) and the elders a Lamb standing, as if slain, having seven horns and seven eyes, which are the seven Spirits of God, sent out into all the earth. Then I looked, and I heard the voice of many angels around the throne and the living creatures and the elders; and the number of them was myriads of myriads, and thousands of thousands, saying with a loud voice, Worthy is the Lamb that was slain to receive power and riches and wisdom and might and honor and glory and blessing."

Revelation 5:4-6, 10-11 (NASB)

Then Jesus again spoke to them, saying, "I am the Light of the world; he who follows Me will not walk in the darkness, but will have the Light of life."

John 8:12 (NASB)

PERSEVERE

Your dream train's off track
Derailed by discouragement
Persevere, press on!

Not that I have already obtained all this, or have already been made perfect, but I press on to take hold of that for which Christ Jesus took hold of me. Brothers, I do not consider myself yet to have taken hold of it. But one thing I do: Forgetting what is behind and straining toward what is ahead, I press on toward the goal to win the prize for which God has called me heavenward in Christ Jesus.

Philippians 3:12-14

Trust in the LORD and do good; dwell in the land and enjoy safe pasture. Delight yourself in the LORD and he will give you the desires of your heart. Commit your way to the LORD; trust in him and he will do this: He will make your righteousness shine like the dawn, the justice of your cause like the noonday sun. Be still before the LORD and wait patiently for him; do not fret when men succeed in their ways, when they carry out their wicked schemes.

Psalm 37:3-7

DIVINATION

"What's my sign" you say?
It's the Holy Spirit's mark
Signed, sealed, delivered

And you also were included in Christ when you heard the word of truth, the gospel of your salvation. Having believed, you were marked in him with a seal, the promised Holy Spirit,

Ephesians 1:13

Do not grieve the Holy Spirit of God, by whom you were sealed for the day of redemption.

Ephesians 4:30 (NASB)

Now it is God who makes both us and you stand firm in Christ. He anointed us, set his seal of ownership on us, and put his Spirit in our hearts as a deposit, guaranteeing what is to come.

2 Corinthians 1:21-22

HOPE FLOATS

I live and I breathe
And so my hope is afloat
This dog's day's coming

Anyone who is among the living has hope —even a live dog is better off than a dead lion!

Ecclesiastes 9:4

For the needy will not always be forgotten, Nor the hope of the afflicted perish forever.

Psalm 9:18 (NASB)

Be joyful in hope, patient in affliction, faithful in prayer.

Romans 12:12

For whatever was written in earlier times was written for our instruction, so that through perseverance and the encouragement of the Scriptures we might have hope.

Romans 15:4 (NASB)

STONES UNCAST

Gazing in mirror
See more guilt than in those judged
Putting down my stones

But when they persisted in asking Him, He straightened up, and said to them, "He who is without sin among you, let him be the first to throw a stone at her."

John 8:7 (NASB)

"Do not judge so that you will not be judged. For in the way you judge, you will be judged; and by your standard of measure, it will be measured to you. Why do you look at the speck that is in your brother's eye, but do not notice the log that is in your own eye? Or how can you say to your brother, 'Let me take the speck out of your eye,' and behold, the log is in your own eye? You hypocrite, first take the log out of your own eye, and then you will see clearly to take the speck out of your brother's eye."

Matthew 7:1-5 (NASB)

RELATIONSHIP

Working through His kids
Is the Lord's favorite way
To express Himself

God can do anything, you know—far more than you could ever imagine or guess or request in your wildest dreams! He does it not by pushing us around but by working within us, his Spirit deeply and gently within us.

Ephesians 3:20 (MSG)

"Let me give you a new command: Love one another. In the same way I loved you, you love one another. This is how everyone will recognize that you are my disciples—when they see the love you have for each other."

John 13:34-35 (MSG)

God, order a peaceful and whole life for us because everything we've done, you've done for us.

Isaiah 26:12 (MSG)

PROTECTION

Strategies devised
Against the children of God
Will all be thwarted

Devise your strategy, but it will be thwarted; propose your plan, but it will not stand, for God is with us.

Isaiah 8:10

But in that coming day no weapon turned against you will succeed. You will silence every voice raised up to accuse you. These benefits are enjoyed by the servants of the Lord; their vindication will come from me. I, the Lord, have spoken!

Isaiah 54:17 (NLT)

The Lord says, "I will rescue those who love me. I will protect those who trust in my name.

Psalm 91:14 (NLT)

CRITICISM

Critical spirit
Cannibal - feeds on itself
Let's starve that sucker!

You may think you can condemn such people, but you are just as bad, and you have no excuse! When you say they are wicked and should be punished, you are condemning yourself, for you who judge others do these very same things. And we know that God, in his justice, will punish anyone who does such things.

Romans 2:1-2 (NLT)

"Do not judge others, and you will not be judged. Do not condemn others, or it will all come back against you. Forgive others, and you will be forgiven. Give, and you will receive. Your gift will return to you in full—pressed down, shaken together to make room for more, running over, and poured into your lap. The amount you give will determine the amount you get back.

Luke 6:37-38 (NLT)

TRUSTWORTHY

I want what He wants
Because what He wants is good
And I can trust Him

'For I know the plans that I have for you,' declares the LORD, 'plans for welfare and not for calamity to give you a future and a hope.'

Jeremiah 29:11 (NASB)

And we know that God causes all things to work together for good to those who love God, to those who are called according to His purpose.

Romans 8:28 (NASB)

Trust in the LORD with all your heart And do not lean on your own understanding. In all your ways acknowledge Him, And He will make your paths straight.

Proverbs 3:5-6 (NASB)

COMMITMENTS

Before you say "yes"
Be careful and prayerful
Overcommitted

An impulsive vow is a trap; later you'll wish you could get out of it.

Proverbs 20:25 (MSG)

Careful planning puts you ahead in the long run; hurry and scurry puts you further behind.

Proverbs 21:5 (MSG)

Don't they know anything, all these impostors? Don't they know they can't get away with this— Treating people like a fast-food meal over which they're too busy to pray?

Psalm 14:4 (MSG)

Slow down. Take a deep breath. What's the hurry? Why wear yourself out? Just what are you after anyway?

Jeremiah 2:25a (MSG)

CROSS BRIDGE

Crossing the chasm
The gap between me and God
The Old Rugged Cross

But God demonstrates His own love toward us, in that while we were yet sinners, Christ died for us.

Romans 5:8 (NASB)

For Christ also died for sins once for all, the just for the unjust, so that He might bring us to God, having been put to death in the flesh, but made alive in the spirit;

1 Peter 3:18 (NASB)

But now in Christ Jesus you who once were far away have been brought near through the blood of Christ. For he himself is our peace, who has made the two one and has destroyed the barrier, the dividing wall of hostility, by abolishing in his flesh the law with its commandments and regulations. His purpose was to create in himself one new man out of the two, thus making peace,

Ephesians 2:13-15

ALL I NEED

Money, fame, power...
All the world holds dear fades fast
You are my portion

But whatever things were gain to me, those things I have counted as loss for the sake of Christ. More than that, I count all things to be loss in view of the surpassing value of knowing Christ Jesus my Lord, for whom I have suffered the loss of all things, and count them but rubbish so that I may gain Christ, and may be found in Him, not having a righteousness of my own derived from the Law, but that which is through faith in Christ, the righteousness which comes from God on the basis of faith,
Philippians 3:7-9 (NASB)

My flesh and my heart may fail, But God is the strength of my heart and my portion forever.
Psalm 73:26 (NASB)

PRUNING

Pruning is painful
But if you want to bear fruit
It's necessary

"I am the true vine, and My Father is the vinedresser. "Every branch in Me that does not bear fruit, He takes away; and every branch that bears fruit, He prunes it so that it may bear more fruit. "You are already clean because of the word which I have spoken to you. "Abide in Me, and I in you. As the branch cannot bear fruit of itself unless it abides in the vine, so neither can you unless you abide in Me. "I am the vine, you are the branches; he who abides in Me and I in him, he bears much fruit, for apart from Me you can do nothing. "If anyone does not abide in Me, he is thrown away as a branch and dries up; and they gather them, and cast them into the fire and they are burned. "If you abide in Me, and My words abide in you, ask whatever you wish, and it will be done for you. "My Father is glorified by this, that you bear much fruit, and so prove to be My disciples."

John 15:1-8 (NASB)

BECAUSE OF HIM

No greater ally
Has religious performance
Than self-righteousness

For it is by grace you have been saved, through faith—and this not from yourselves, it is the gift of God— not by works, so that no one can boast.

Ephesians 2:8-9

For everyone has sinned; we all fall short of God's glorious standard. Yet God, with undeserved kindness, declares that we are righteous. He did this through Christ Jesus when he freed us from the penalty for our sins.

Romans 3:23-24 (NLT)

Yet we know that a person is made right with God by faith in Jesus Christ, not by obeying the law.

Galatians 2:16 (NLT)

INTROSPECTION

Check your responses
Anger usually means
Something is broken

Post this at all the intersections, dear friends: Lead with your ears, follow up with your tongue, and let anger straggle along in the rear. God's righteousness doesn't grow from human anger. So throw all spoiled virtue and cancerous evil in the garbage. In simple humility, let our gardener, God, landscape you with the Word, making a salvation-garden of your life.

James 1:19-21 (MSG)

A gentle response defuses anger, but a sharp tongue kindles a temper-fire.

Proverbs 15:1 (MSG)

A fool gives full vent to his anger, but a wise man keeps himself under control.

Proverbs 29:11

MONARCHY

Give me monarchy
Where righteousness is the rule
Such a King's coming

But he says to the Son, You're God, and on the throne for good; your rule makes everything right. You love it when things are right; you hate it when things are wrong. That is why God, your God, poured fragrant oil on your head, Marking you out as king, far above your dear companions.

Hebrews 1:8-9 (MSG)

Look, a righteous king is coming! And honest princes will rule under him. Each one will be like a shelter from the wind and a refuge from the storm, like streams of water in the desert and the shadow of a great rock in a parched land. Then everyone who has eyes will be able to see the truth, and everyone who has ears will be able to hear it.

Isaiah 32:1-3 (NLT)

CHANGE

It's pretty boring
Living in your comfort zones
Change is a God thing

Be alert, be present. I'm about to do something brand-new. It's bursting out! Don't you see it? There it is! I'm making a road through the desert, rivers in the badlands.

Isaiah 43:19 (MSG)

And He who sits on the throne said, "Behold, I am making all things new" And He said, "Write, for these words are faithful and true."

Revelation 21:5 (NASB)

Then Jesus gave them this illustration: "No one tears a piece of cloth from a new garment and uses it to patch an old garment. For then the new garment would be ruined, and the new patch wouldn't even match the old garment. "And no one puts new wine into old wineskins. For the new wine would burst the wineskins, spilling the wine and ruining the skins. New wine must be stored in new wineskins.

Luke 5:36-38 (NLT)

FATHER'S HEART

Coming back to Dad
The Prodigal parable
His arms are open

So he returned home to his father. And while he was still a long way off, his father saw him coming. Filled with love and compassion, he ran to his son, embraced him, and kissed him. His son said to him, 'Father, I have sinned against both heaven and you, and I am no longer worthy of being called your son.' But his father said to the servants, 'Quick! Bring the finest robe in the house and put it on him. Get a ring for his finger and sandals for his feet. And kill the calf we have been fattening. We must celebrate with a feast, for this son of mine was dead and has now returned to life. He was lost, but now he is found.' So the party began.

Luke 15:20-24 (NLT)

DISCIPLINE

Why are good habits
So much harder to be formed
Than not so good ones?

I do not understand what I do. For what I want to do I do not do, but what I hate I do. And if I do what I do not want to do, I agree that the law is good. As it is, it is no longer I myself who do it, but it is sin living in me. I know that nothing good lives in me, that is, in my sinful nature. For I have the desire to do what is good, but I cannot carry it out. For what I do is not the good I want to do; no, the evil I do not want to do—this I keep on doing.

Romans 8:15-19

For God did not give us a spirit of timidity, but a spirit of power, of love and of self-discipline.

2 Timothy 1:7

HOLY SPIRIT

Holy Spirit come
To be the me I'm to be
I need more of You

And we, who with unveiled faces all reflect the Lord's glory, are being transformed into his likeness with ever-increasing glory, which comes from the Lord, who is the Spirit.

2 Corinthians 3:18

"Don't bargain with God. Be direct. Ask for what you need. This is not a cat-and-mouse, hide-and-seek game we're in. If your little boy asks for a serving of fish, do you scare him with a live snake on his plate? If your little girl asks for an egg, do you trick her with a spider? As bad as you are, you wouldn't think of such a thing—you're at least decent to your own children. And don't you think the Father who conceived you in love will give the Holy Spirit when you ask him?"

Luke 11:10-13 (MSG)

DEEP ✢ WIDE

Immeasurable
The height and width, length and depth
Of the love of God

My response is to get down on my knees before the Father, this magnificent Father who parcels out all heaven and earth. I ask him to strengthen you by his Spirit—not a brute strength but a glorious inner strength—that Christ will live in you as you open the door and invite him in. And I ask him that with both feet planted firmly on love, you'll be able to take in with all followers of Jesus the extravagant dimensions of Christ's love. Reach out and experience the breadth! Test its length! Plumb the depths! Rise to the heights! Live full lives, full in the fullness of God.

Ephesians 3:16-19 (MSG)

God told them, "I've never quit loving you and never will. Expect love, love, and more love!

Jeremiah 31:3 (MSG)

AFFIRMATION

Need affirmation?
Look not to man but to God
He has what you need

While he was still speaking, a bright cloud overshadowed them, and behold, a voice out of the cloud said, "This is My beloved Son, with whom I am well-pleased; listen to Him!

Matthew 17:5 (NASB)

Fire tests the purity of silver and gold, but a person is tested by being praised.

Proverbs 27:21 (NLT)

How great is the love the Father has lavished on us, that we should be called children of God! And that is what we are!

1 John 3:1a

GIFTS

Our sons and daughters
Such precious gifts from above
Celebrate children

Behold, children are a gift of the LORD, The fruit of the womb is a reward.

Psalm 127:3 (NASB)

He gives childless couples a family, gives them joy as the parents of children. Hallelujah!

Psalm 113:9 (MSG)

For this boy I prayed, and the LORD has given me my petition which I asked of Him.

1 Samuel 1:27 (NASB)

"Let these children alone. Don't get between them and me. These children are the kingdom's pride and joy. Mark this: Unless you accept God's kingdom in the simplicity of a child, you'll never get in."

Luke 18:16-17 (MSG)

SURGERY

Childhood pain and loss
Built up walls around my heart
That must be torn down

He heals the brokenhearted And binds up their wounds.
Psalm 147:3 (NASB)

Behold, You desire truth in the innermost being, And in the hidden part You will make me know wisdom.
Psalm 51:6 (NASB)

Even if my father and mother abandon me, the Lord will hold me close.
Psalm 27:10 (NLT)

Come close to God, and God will come close to you.
James 4:8a (NLT)

Relax, everything's going to be all right; rest, everything's coming together; open your hearts, love is on the way!
Jude 1:1b (MSG)

GOLDEN RULE

Feeling down in the dumps?
Encourage someone today
Watch your spirit's lift

Here is a simple rule of thumb for behavior: Ask yourself what you want people to do for you; then grab the initiative and do it for them!

Luke 6:31 (MSG)

And let us not neglect our meeting together, as some people do, but encourage one another, especially now that the day of his return is drawing near.

Hebrews 10:5 (NLT)

So encourage each other and build each other up, just as you are already doing.

1 Thessalonians 5:11 (NLT)

Kind words heal and help;

Proverbs 15:4a (MSG)

RAGS TO RICHES

Homo Sapiens
Inauspicious beginning
Glorious finish

"Who told you that you were naked?" the Lord God asked. "Have you eaten from the tree whose fruit I commanded you not to eat?"

Genesis 3:11 (NLT)

"God himself will be with them. He will wipe every tear from their eyes, and there will be no more death or sorrow or crying or pain. All these things are gone forever." And the one sitting on the throne said, "Look, I am making everything new!" And then he said to me, "Write this down, for what I tell you is trustworthy and true." And he also said, "It is finished! I am the Alpha and the Omega—the Beginning and the End. To all who are thirsty I will give freely from the springs of the water of life. All who are victorious will inherit all these blessings, and I will be their God, and they will be my children.

Revelation 21:3b-7 (NLT)

RADICAL

If you're really bored
Try hanging out with Jesus
Life of this party

The thief comes only to steal and kill and destroy; I came that they may have life, and have it abundantly.

John 10:10 (NASB)

Your life is a journey you must travel with a deep conscious-ness of God. It cost God plenty to get you out of that dead-end, empty-headed life you grew up in. He paid with Christ's sacred blood, you know. He died like an unblemished, sacrificial lamb. And this was no afterthought. Even though it has only lately—at the end of the ages—become public knowledge, God always knew he was going to do this for you. It's because of this sacrificed Messiah, whom God then raised from the dead and glorified, that you trust God, that you know you have a future in God.

1 Peter 1:18-21 (MSG)

PURPOSE

What is that ringing?
The call of God on your life
Hope you'll answer it

For we are God's workmanship, created in Christ Jesus to do good works, which God prepared in advance for us to do.

Ephesians 2:10

However, as it is written: "No eye has seen, no ear has heard, no mind has conceived what God has prepared for those who love him."

1 Corinthians 2:9

"For I know the plans I have for you," declares the LORD, "plans to prosper you and not to harm you, plans to give you hope and a future.

Jeremiah 29:11

The LORD will fulfill his purpose for me; your love, O LORD, endures forever— do not abandon the works of your hands.

Psalm 138:8

OBEDIENCE

I've a real talent
For wasting time, bad choices
My will is a won't

What I don't understand about myself is that I decide one way, but then I act another, doing things I absolutely despise. So if I can't be trusted to figure out what is best for myself and then do it, it becomes obvious that God's command is necessary. But I need something more! For if I know the law but still can't keep it, and if the power of sin within me keeps sabotaging my best intentions, I obviously need help! I realize that I don't have what it takes. I can will it, but I can't do it. I decide to do good, but I don't really do it; I decide not to do bad, but then I do it anyway. My decisions, such as they are, don't result in actions. Something has gone wrong deep within me and gets the better of me every time.

Romans 7:15-20 (MSG)

And this is love: that we walk in obedience to his commands.

2 John 1:6a

IMAGE

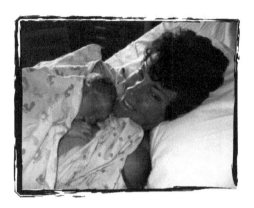

Man in His image
Creation's punctuation
Exclamation point

Then God said, "Let Us make man in Our image, according to Our likeness; and let them rule over the fish of the sea and over the birds of the sky and over the cattle and over all the earth, and over every creeping thing that creeps on the earth." God created man in His own image, in the image of God He created him; male and female He created them.

Genesis 1:26-27 (NASB)

When I consider Your heavens, the work of Your fingers, The moon and the stars, which You have ordained; What is man that You take thought of him, And the son of man that You care for him? Yet You have made him a little lower than God, And You crown him with glory and majesty!

Psalm 8:3-5 (NASB)

HARD ROADS

Times are getting tough
Discouragement, fear stalk us
Faith, hope persevere

Even though I walk through the valley of the shadow of death,
I will fear no evil, for you are with me; your rod and your staff,
they comfort me.

Psalm 23:4

The LORD is my light and my salvation— whom shall I fear?
The LORD is the stronghold of my life— of whom shall I be
afraid? When evil men advance against me to devour my flesh,
when my enemies and my foes attack me, they will stumble and
fall. Though an army besiege me, my heart will not fear; though
war break out against me, even then will I be confident.

Psalm 27:1-3

Blessed is the man who perseveres under trial, because when he
has stood the test, he will receive the crown of life that God has
promised to those who love him.

James 1:12

TRUE SOURCE

Sex, work, thrills, drugs, booze...
Everyone looking for love
Counterfeit culture

You're addicted to thrills? What an empty life! The pursuit of pleasure is never satisfied."

Proverbs 21:17 (MSG)

Ephraim is finished with gods that are no-gods. From now on I'm the one who answers and satisfies him. I am like a luxuriant fruit tree. Everything you need is to be found in me.

Hosea 14:8 (MSG)

God, the one and only— I'll wait as long as he says. Everything I need comes from him, so why not? He's solid rock under my feet, breathing room for my soul, An impregnable castle: I'm set for life.

Psalm 62:1-2 (MSG)

SURRENDER

"I surrender all"
It's been sung a million times
But only done once

Therefore be imitators of God, as beloved children; and walk in love, just as Christ also loved you and gave Himself up for us, an offering and a sacrifice to God as a fragrant aroma.

Ephesians 5:1-2 (NASB)

For there is one God, and one mediator also between God and men, the man Christ Jesus, who gave Himself as a ransom for all, the testimony given at the proper time.

1 Timothy 2:5-6 (NASB)

I am the good shepherd; the good shepherd lays down His life for the sheep.

John 10:11 (NASB)

VISIBILITY

God is on a roll
Everything's going His way
You just can't see it

Furthermore, because we are united with Christ, we have received an inheritance from God, for he chose us in advance, and he makes everything work out according to his plan.

Ephesians 1:11 (NLT)

Oh, how great are God's riches and wisdom and knowledge! How impossible it is for us to understand his decisions and his ways!

Romans 11:33 (NLT)

I have a plan for the whole earth, a hand of judgment upon all the nations. The Lord of Heaven's Armies has spoken— who can change his plans? When his hand is raised, who can stop him?"

Isaiah 14:26-27 (NLT)

STORM WARNING

Oh for a siren
Giving me advance warning
When storms of life near

Therefore everyone who hears these words of Mine and acts on them, may be compared to a wise man who built his house on the rock. And the rain fell, and the floods came, and the winds blew and slammed against that house; and yet it did not fall, for it had been founded on the rock.

Matthew 7:24-25 (NASB)

For You have been a defense for the helpless, A defense for the needy in his distress, A refuge from the storm, a shade from the heat; For the breath of the ruthless Is like a rain storm against a wall.

Isaiah 25:4 (NASB)

These things I have spoken to you, so that in Me you may have peace In the world you have tribulation, but take courage; I have overcome the world.

John 16:33 (NASB)

FREEDOM

Bitterness bondage
Unforgiveness enslavement
Let love break the chains

Therefore, as God's chosen people, holy and dearly loved, clothe yourselves with compassion, kindness, humility, gentleness and patience. Bear with each other and forgive whatever grievances you may have against one another. Forgive as the Lord forgave you. And over all these virtues put on love, which binds them all together in perfect unity.

Colossians 3:12-14

Get rid of all bitterness, rage and anger, brawling and slander, along with every form of malice. Be kind and compassionate to one another, forgiving each other, just as in Christ God forgave you.

Ephesians 4:31-32

If it is possible, as far as it depends on you, live at peace with everyone.

Romans 12:18

MORTALITY

Rich, poor, wise, foolish
Ugly or drop-dead gorgeous
We will all drop dead

And just as each person is destined to die once and after that comes judgment, so also Christ died once for all time as a sacrifice to take away the sins of many people. He will come again, not to deal with our sins, but to bring salvation to all who are eagerly waiting for him.

Hebrews 9:27-28 (NLT)

Lord, remind me how brief my time on earth will be. Remind me that my days are numbered— how fleeting my life is. You have made my life no longer than the width of my hand. My entire lifetime is just a moment to you; at best, each of us is but a breath.

Psalm 39:3-4 (NLT)

DEATH TRAP

Sultry seductress
Tantalizes lust within
Fatal attraction

So, friends, listen to me, take these words of mine most serious-
ly. Don't fool around with a woman like that; don't even stroll
through her neighborhood. Countless victims come under her
spell; she's the death of many a poor man. She runs a halfway
house to hell, fits you out with a shroud and a coffin.

Proverbs 7:24-27 (MSG)

You know the next commandment pretty well, too: 'Don't go to
bed with another's spouse.' But don't think you've preserved your
virtue simply by staying out of bed. Your heart can be corrupted
by lust even quicker than your body. Those leering looks you
think nobody notices—they also corrupt.

Matthew 5:27-28 (MSG)

OUTLOOK

Life's not what happens
It's how you respond to it
Opposite spirit

Be joyful in hope, patient in affliction, faithful in prayer... Bless those who persecute you; bless and do not curse... Do not repay anyone evil for evil... Do not be overcome by evil, but overcome evil with good.

Romans 12:12,14,17a,21

But I say to you who hear, love your enemies, do good to those who hate you, bless those who curse you, pray for those who mistreat you.

Luke 6:27-28 (NASB)

A cheerful disposition is good for your health; gloom and doom leave you bone-tired.

Proverbs 17:22 (MSG)

AFFECTION

No end to His love
No limit to His patience
God's waiting for you

But for that very reason I was shown mercy so that in me, the worst of sinners, Christ Jesus might display his unlimited patience as an example for those who would believe on him and receive eternal life.

1 Timothy 1:16

This is good and acceptable in the sight of God our Savior, who desires all men to be saved and to come to the knowledge of the truth.

1 Timothy 2:3-4 (NASB)

And I ask him that with both feet planted firmly on love, you'll be able to take in with all followers of Jesus the extravagant dimensions of Christ's love. Reach out and experience the breadth! Test its length! Plumb the depths!

Ephesians 3:17b-18 (MSG)

READY

Wherever it is
You're wanting me to go Lord
Send me on my way

And Jesus came up and spoke to them, saying, "All authority has been given to Me in heaven and on earth. Go therefore and make disciples of all the nations, baptizing them in the name of the Father and the Son and the Holy Spirit, teaching them to observe all that I commanded you; and lo, I am with you always, even to the end of the age."

Matthew 28:18-20 (NASB)

Then I heard the voice of the Lord, saying, "Whom shall I send, and who will go for Us?" Then I said, "Here am I. Send me!"

Isaiah 6:8 (NASB)

Therefore, come now, and I will send you to Pharaoh, so that you may bring My people, the sons of Israel, out of Egypt.

Exodus 3:10 (NASB)

ONE COMMAND

Knowing what is right
But not doing it, that's sin
Love's not optional

Remember, it is sin to know what you ought to do and then not do it.

James 4:17 (NLT)

For the whole law can be summed up in this one command: "Love your neighbor as yourself."

Galatians 5:14 (NLT)

For the commandments say, "You must not commit adultery. You must not murder. You must not steal. You must not covet." These—and other such commandments—are summed up in this one commandment: "Love your neighbor as yourself."

Romans 13:9 (NLT)

This is my commandment: Love each other in the same way I have loved you.

John 15:12 (NLT)

JUDGEMENT DAY

**Some hunt for the truth
Some are not interested
But all will face Him**

Just as man is destined to die once, and after that to face judgment, so Christ was sacrificed once to take away the sins of many people; and he will appear a second time, not to bear sin, but to bring salvation to those who are waiting for him.

Hebrews 9:27-28

It is written: " 'As surely as I live,' says the Lord, 'every knee will bow before me; every tongue will confess to God.' " So then, each of us will give an account of himself to God.

Romans 14:11-12

Jesus answered, "I am the way and the truth and the life. No one comes to the Father except through me."

John 14:6

SHINE

Beacons: burn brightly!
To the ships lost in the fog
Your light could save them

"You are the light of the world—like a city on a hilltop that cannot be hidden. No one lights a lamp and then puts it under a basket. Instead, a lamp is placed on a stand, where it gives light to everyone in the house. In the same way, let your good deeds shine out for all to see, so that everyone will praise your heavenly Father."

Matthew 5:14-16 (NLT)

God sent a man, John the Baptist, to tell about the light so that everyone might believe because of his testimony. John himself was not the light; he was simply a witness to tell about the light. The one who is the true light, who gives light to everyone, was coming into the world.

John 1:6-9 (NLT)

INTUITION

God's a paradox
He defies intuition
But children get Him

At that time Jesus said, "I praise You, Father, Lord of heaven and earth, that You have hidden these things from the wise and intelligent and have revealed them to infants.

Matthew 11:25 (NASB)

Have you ever come on anything quite like this extravagant generosity of God, this deep, deep wisdom? It's way over our heads. We'll never figure it out. Is there anyone around who can explain God? Anyone smart enough to tell him what to do? Anyone who has done him such a huge favor that God has to ask his advice? Everything comes from him; Everything happens through him; Everything ends up in him. Always glory! Always praise! Yes. Yes. Yes.

Romans 11:33-36 (MSG)

REDEEMER

His splendor displayed
In reclamation projects
I am one of them

The Spirit of the Sovereign LORD is on me, because the
LORD has anointed me to preach good news to the poor. He
has sent me to bind up the brokenhearted, to proclaim freedom
for the captives and release from darkness for the prisoners,
to proclaim the year of the LORD's favor and the day of ven-
geance of our God, to comfort all who mourn, and provide
for those who grieve in Zion— to bestow on them a crown of
beauty instead of ashes, the oil of gladness instead of mourning, and a garment of praise instead of a spirit of despair. They
will be called oaks of righteousness, a planting of the LORD
for the display of his splendor.

Isaiah 61:1-3

He lifted me out of the slimy pit, out of the mud and mire; he set
my feet on a rock and gave me a firm place to stand.

Psalm 40:2

BATTLEFIELD

Down in the trenches
Prayer's a powerful weapon
Hand in hand combat

For though we live in the world, we do not wage war as the
world does. The weapons we fight with are not the weapons of
the world. On the contrary, they have divine power to demolish
strongholds. We demolish arguments and every pretension that
sets itself up against the knowledge of God, and we take captive
every thought to make it obedient to Christ.

2 Corinthians 10:3-5

Therefore, confess your sins to one another, and pray for one
another so that you may be healed. The effective prayer of a righteous man can accomplish much.

James 5:16 (NASB)

Though one may be overpowered, two can defend themselves. A
cord of three strands is not quickly broken.

Ecclesiastes 4:12

HELPING HAND

*We all need someone
Who picks us up when we fall
And renews our hope*

God gives a hand to those down on their luck, gives a fresh start to those ready to quit.

Psalm 145:14 (MSG)

God-loyal people don't stay down long; Soon they're up on their feet, while the wicked end up flat on their faces.

Proverbs 24:16 (MSG)

If one falls down, his friend can help him up. But pity the man who falls and has no one to help him up!

Ecclesiastes 4:10

So encourage each other and build each other up, just as you are already doing.

1 Thessalonians 5:11 (NLT)

SELF

Me, Myself and I
Foremost in the thoughts of man
Lord, help me change mine

If you've gotten anything at all out of following Christ, if his love has made any difference in your life, if being in a community of the Spirit means anything to you, if you have a heart, if you care— then do me a favor: Agree with each other, love each other, be deep-spirited friends. Don't push your way to the front; don't sweet-talk your way to the top. Put yourself aside, and help others get ahead. Don't be obsessed with getting your own advantage. Forget yourselves long enough to lend a helping hand. Think of yourselves the way Christ Jesus thought of himself. He had equal status with God but didn't think so much of himself that he had to cling to the advantages of that status no matter what. Not at all. When the time came, he set aside the privileges of deity and took on the status of a slave, became human! Having become human, he stayed human. It was an incredibly humbling process. He didn't claim special privileges. Instead, he lived a selfless, obedient life and then died a selfless, obedient death—and the worst kind of death at that—a crucifixion.

Philippians 2:1-8 (MSG)

WORD BALM

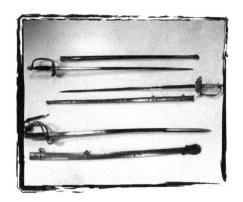

Reckless, piercing words
Swords run through, leaving regret
Wise tongues bring healing

Reckless words pierce like a sword, but the tongue of the wise brings healing.

Proverbs 12:18

Do not let any unwholesome talk come out of your mouths, but only what is helpful for building others up according to their needs, that it may benefit those who listen.

Ephesians 4:29

It only takes a spark, remember, to set off a forest fire. A careless or wrongly placed word out of your mouth can do that. By our speech we can ruin the world, turn harmony to chaos, throw mud on a reputation, send the whole world up in smoke and go up in smoke with it, smoke right from the pit of hell.

James 3:5-6 (MSG)

VESSELS

How can God use you?
Endless possibilities!
Beyond conception

Now to him who is able to do immeasurably more than all we
ask or imagine, according to his power that is at work within us,
Ephesians 3:20

For I can do everything through Christ, who gives me strength.
Philippians 4:13 (NLT)

Then the Lord turned to him and said, "Go with the strength
you have, and rescue Israel from the Midianites. I am sending
you!" "But Lord," Gideon replied, "how can I rescue Israel? My
clan is the weakest in the whole tribe of Manasseh, and I am the
least in my entire family!" The Lord said to him, "I will be with
you. And you will destroy the Midianites as if you were fighting
against one man."
Judges 6:14-16 (NLT)

THANKFULNESS

Lord, create in me
A gratitude attitude
A hopeful mindset

But as for me, I will always have hope; I will praise you more and more.

Psalm 71:14

and hope does not disappoint, because the love of God has been poured out within our hearts through the Holy Spirit who was given to us.

Romans 5:5 (NASB)

Let the peace of Christ rule in your hearts, to which indeed you were called in one body; and be thankful. Let the word of Christ richly dwell within you, with all wisdom teaching and admonishing one another with psalms and hymns and spiritual songs, singing with thankfulness in your hearts to God. Whatever you do in word or deed, do all in the name of the Lord Jesus, giving thanks through Him to God the Father.

Colossians 3:15-17 (NASB)

PATIENT PAPA

I bumble, stumble
God never gives up on me
Patience unending

Here's a word you can take to heart and depend on: Jesus Christ came into the world to save sinners. I'm proof—Public Sinner Number One—of someone who could never have made it apart from sheer mercy. And now he shows me off—evidence of his endless patience—to those who are right on the edge of trusting him forever.

1 Timothy 1:15-16 (MSG)

Rend your heart and not your garments. Return to the LORD your God, for he is gracious and compassionate, slow to anger and abounding in love, and he relents from sending calamity.

Joel 2:13

RIGHT & WRONGED

Those who have been wronged
Oft have strong need to be right
No healing there though

The Spirit of the Sovereign Lord is upon me, for the Lord has anointed me to bring good news to the poor. He has sent me to comfort the brokenhearted and to proclaim that captives will be released and prisoners will be freed.

Isaiah 61:1 (NLT)

Those who have been ransomed by the Lord will return. They will enter Jerusalem singing, crowned with everlasting joy. Sorrow and mourning will disappear, and they will be filled with joy and gladness.

Isaiah 35:10 (NLT)

The Lord is close to the brokenhearted; he rescues those whose spirits are crushed.

Psalm 34:18 (NLT)

LORD OF HOSTS

Eyes of blazing fire
White-horsed armies of heaven
"Shock and Awe" campaign

Then I saw heaven opened, and a white horse was standing there. Its rider was named Faithful and True, for he judges fairly and wages a righteous war. His eyes were like flames of fire, and on his head were many crowns. A name was written on him that no one understood except himself. He wore a robe dipped in blood, and his title was the Word of God. The armies of heaven, dressed in the finest of pure white linen, followed him on white horses. From his mouth came a sharp sword to strike down the nations. He will rule them with an iron rod. He will release the fierce wrath of God, the Almighty, like juice flowing from a winepress. On his robe at his thigh was written this title: King of all kings and Lord of all lords.

Revelation 19:11-16 (NLT)

PREPARATION

Seat belt lights are on
Turbulence awaits us all
Will you be shaken?

So be on your guard; I have told you everything ahead of time. "But in those days, following that distress, " 'the sun will be darkened, and the moon will not give its light; the stars will fall from the sky, and the heavenly bodies will be shaken.' "At that time men will see the Son of Man coming in clouds with great power and glory. And he will send his angels and gather his elect from the four winds, from the ends of the earth to the ends of the heavens.

Mark 13:23-27

I have set the LORD always before me. Because he is at my right hand, I will not be shaken.

Psalm 16:8

PROXIMITY

When life bombards me
The shelter of His presence
Deflects the shrapnel

How great is Your goodness, Which You have stored up for those who fear You, Which You have wrought for those who take refuge in You, Before the sons of men! You hide them in the secret place of Your presence from the conspiracies of man; You keep them secretly in a shelter from the strife of tongues.

Psalm 31:19-20 (NASB)

For he will rescue you from every trap and protect you from deadly disease. He will cover you with his feathers. He will shelter you with his wings. His faithful promises are your armor and protection. Do not be afraid of the terrors of the night, nor the arrow that flies in the day. Do not dread the disease that stalks in darkness, nor the disaster that strikes at midday.

Psalm 91:3-6 (NLT)

24/7

Thank God it's Friday
Is not observed in heaven
God works on weekends

Jesus said to them, "My Father is always at his work to this very day, and I, too, am working."

John 5:17

I look up to the mountains— does my help come from there? My help comes from the Lord, who made heaven and earth! He will not let you stumble; the one who watches over you will not slumber. Indeed, he who watches over Israel never slumbers or sleeps. The Lord himself watches over you! The Lord stands beside you as your protective shade. The sun will not harm you by day, nor the moon at night. The Lord keeps you from all harm and watches over your life. The Lord keeps watch over you as you come and go, both now and forever.

Psalm 121 (NLT)

WAITING

Promises of God
Are fulfilled in His timing
Hold off and hold on

We were given this hope when we were saved. (If we already have something, we don't need to hope for it. But if we look forward to something we don't yet have, we must wait patiently and confidently.)

Romans 8:24-25 (NLT)

Against all hope, Abraham in hope believed and so became the father of many nations, just as it had been said to him, "So shall your offspring be." Without weakening in his faith, he faced the fact that his body was as good as dead—since he was about a hundred years old—and that Sarah's womb was also dead. Yet he did not waver through unbelief regarding the promise of God, but was strengthened in his faith and gave glory to God, being fully persuaded that that God had power to do what he had promised.

Romans 4:18-21

COMFORT

Suffering comfort
His promise preserves my life
My hope is in Him

Remember your word to your servant, for you have given me hope. My comfort in my suffering is this: Your promise preserves my life.

Psalm 119:49-50

Not only so, but we also rejoice in our sufferings, because we know that suffering produces perseverance; perseverance, character; and character, hope. And hope does not disappoint us, because God has poured out his love into our hearts by the Holy Spirit, whom he has given us.

Romans 5:3-5 (NASB)

For just as the sufferings of Christ are ours in abundance, so also our comfort is abundant through Christ.

2 Corinthians 1:5 (NASB)

CONTENTMENT

Live in the moment
Even if the moment stinks
Life doesn't have to

I'm glad in God, far happier than you would ever guess—happy that you're again showing such strong concern for me. Not that you ever quit praying and thinking about me. You just had no chance to show it. Actually, I don't have a sense of needing anything personally. I've learned by now to be quite content whatever my circumstances. I'm just as happy with little as with much, with much as with little. I've found the recipe for being happy whether full or hungry, hands full or hands empty. What-ever I have, wherever I am, I can make it through anything in the One who makes me who I am. I don't mean that your help didn't mean a lot to me—it did. It was a beautiful thing that you came alongside me in my troubles.

Philippians 4:10-14 (MSG)

DAILY DYING

Dying to yourself
A more rigorous journey
You will never know

Then Jesus said to His disciples, "If anyone wishes to come after Me, he must deny himself, and take up his cross and follow Me. "For whoever wishes to save his life will lose it; but whoever loses his life for My sake will find it. "For what will it profit a man if he gains the whole world and forfeits his soul? Or what will a man give in exchange for his soul?

Matthew 16:24-26 (NASB)

Since, then, we do not have the excuse of ignorance, every-thing—and I do mean everything—connected with that old way of life has to go. It's rotten through and through. Get rid of it! And then take on an entirely new way of life—a God-fashioned life, a life renewed from the inside and working itself into your conduct as God accurately reproduces his character in you.

Ephesians 4:22-24 (MSG)

DAILY BREAD

All you need today
Waiting for you in God's Word
Release the power

Man does not live on bread alone, but on every word that comes from the mouth of God. Matthew 4:4b

The Son is the radiance of God's glory and the exact representation of his being, sustaining all things by his powerful word.

Hebrews 1:3a

For the word of God is living and active and sharper than any two-edged sword, and piercing as far as the division of soul and spirit, of both joints and marrow, and able to judge the thoughts and intentions of the heart.

Hebrews 4:12 (NASB)

It is the Spirit who gives life; the flesh profits nothing; the words that I have spoken to you are spirit and are life.

John 6:63 (NASB)

DEDICATION

Lord, please have Your way
With my heart, hands, feet, focus
Spirit filled and led

I know, O LORD, that a man's way is not in himself, Nor is it in a man who walks to direct his steps.

Jeremiah 10:23 (NASB)

I am God, your God, who teaches you how to live right and well.

Isaiah 48:17 (MSG)

But you are not controlled by your sinful nature. You are controlled by the Spirit if you have the Spirit of God living in you.

Romans 8:9 (NLT)

The mind of man plans his way, But the LORD directs his steps.

Proverbs 16:9 (NASB)

UNITY

Camaraderie
Rarely found between churches
Much to God's chagrin

I'm praying not only for them But also for those who will believe in me Because of them and their witness about me. The goal is for all of them to become one heart and mind— Just as you, Father, are in me and I in you, So they might be one heart and mind with us. Then the world might believe that you, in fact, sent me.

John 17:22-23 (MSG)

May God, who gives this patience and encouragement, help you live in complete harmony with each other, as is fitting for followers of Christ Jesus. Then all of you can join together with one voice, giving praise and glory to God, the Father of our Lord Jesus Christ.

Romans 15:5-6 (NLT)

NATURE CHORUS

Creation singing
Seas, hills, trees join the chorus
Vibrant harmonies

Let the heavens be glad, and let the earth rejoice; Let the sea roar, and all it contains; Let the field exult, and all that is in it. Then all the trees of the forest will sing for joy Before the LORD, for He is coming, For He is coming to judge the earth. He will judge the world in righteousness And the peoples in His faithfulness.

Psalm 96:11-13 (NASB)

Praise him, skies above! Praise him, vapors high above the clouds! Let every created thing give praise to the Lord, for he issued his command, and they came into being. ~ Praise the Lord from the earth, you creatures of the ocean depths, mountains and all hills, fruit trees and all cedars, ~ Let them all praise the name of the Lord. For his name is very great; his glory towers over the earth and heaven!

Psalm 148:4-5,7-9,13

FOR HIM

If not for the Lord
Then our labor is in vain
Keep up the God work

Whatever you do, do your work heartily, as for the Lord rather than for men,

Colossians 3:23 (NASB)

Unless the LORD builds the house, They labor in vain who build it; Unless the LORD guards the city, The watchman keeps awake in vain.

Psalm 127:1 (NASB)

The King will answer and say to them, 'Truly I say to you, to the extent that you did it to one of these brothers of Mine, even the least of them, you did it to Me.'

Matthew 25:40 (NASB)

But store up for yourselves treasures in heaven, where neither moth nor rust destroys, and where thieves do not break in or steal;

Matthew 6:20 (NASB)

FRIEND OF SINNNERS

They hated Jesus
For consorting with "sinners"
Glass-house Pharisees

Later when Jesus was eating supper at Matthew's house with his close followers, a lot of disreputable characters came and joined them. When the Pharisees saw him keeping this kind of company, they had a fit, and lit into Jesus' followers. "What kind of example is this from your Teacher, acting cozy with crooks and riffraff?" Jesus, overhearing, shot back, "Who needs a doctor: the healthy or the sick? Go figure out what this Scripture means: 'I'm after mercy, not religion.' I'm here to invite outsiders, not coddle insiders."

Matthew 9:10-14 (MSG)

"The Son of Man came eating and drinking, and you say, 'Here is a glutton and a drunkard, a friend of tax collectors and "sinners." ' But wisdom is proved right by all her children."

Luke 7:34-35

LIGHT

If not for Christmas
The hopes of mankind would be
Depressingly dim

The people walking in darkness have seen a great light; on those living in the land of the shadow of death a light has dawned.

Isaiah 9:2

Then Jesus again spoke to them, saying, "I am the Light of the world; he who follows Me will not walk in the darkness, but will have the Light of life."

John 8:12 (NASB)

In those days you were living apart from Christ. You were excluded from citizenship among the people of Israel, and you did not know the covenant promises God had made to them. You lived in this world without God and without hope.

Ephesians 2:12 (NLT)

WONDERFUL LIFE

George Bailey learned it
By the end of the movie
Life's SO worth living!

The thief's purpose is to steal and kill and destroy. My purpose is to give them a rich and satisfying life.

John 10:10 (NLT)

Seize life! Eat bread with gusto, Drink wine with a robust heart. Oh yes—God takes pleasure in your pleasure! Dress festively every morning. Don't skimp on colors and scarves. Relish life with the spouse you love Each and every day of your precarious life. Each day is God's gift. It's all you get in exchange For the hard work of staying alive. Make the most of each one! Whatever turns up, grab it and do it. And heartily! This is your last and only chance at it,

Ecclesiastes 9:7-9 (MSG)

KNOCK KNOCK

God does not barge in
Your heart opens from inside
Why not let Him in?

Look! I stand at the door and knock. If you hear my voice and open the door, I will come in, and we will share a meal together as friends.

Revelation 3:20 (NLT)

Jerusalem, Jerusalem, who kills the prophets and stones those who are sent to her! How often I wanted to gather your children together, the way a hen gathers her chicks under her wings, and you were unwilling.

Matthew 23:37 (NASB)

I was asleep but my heart was awake. A voice! My beloved was knocking: 'Open to me, my sister, my darling, My dove, my perfect one! For my head is drenched with dew, My locks with the damp of the night.'

Song of Solomon 5:2 (NASB)

LOVED

At my very worst
As ugly as I can get
God loves me right there

But God demonstrates His own love toward us, in that while we were yet sinners, Christ died for us.

Romans 5:8 (NASB)

Love is patient and kind. Love is not jealous or boastful or proud or rude. It does not demand its own way. It is not irritable, and it keeps no record of being wronged.

1 Corinthians 13:4-5 (NLT)

And I am convinced that nothing can ever separate us from God's love. Neither death nor life, neither angels nor demons, neither our fears for today nor our worries about tomorrow—not even the powers of hell can separate us from God's love. No power in the sky above or in the earth below—indeed, nothing in all creation will ever be able to separate us from the love of God that is revealed in Christ Jesus our Lord.

Romans 8:38-39 (NLT)

WAR

Don't want what I do
Then I don't do what I want
War! Forces compete

And I know that nothing good lives in me, that is, in my sinful nature. I want to do what is right, but I can't. I want to do what is good, but I don't. I don't want to do what is wrong, but I do it anyway. But if I do what I don't want to do, I am not really the one doing wrong; it is sin living in me that does it.

I have discovered this principle of life—that when I want to do what is right, I inevitably do what is wrong. I love God's law with all my heart. But there is another power within me that is at war with my mind. This power makes me a slave to the sin that is still within me. Oh, what a miserable person I am! Who will free me from this life that is dominated by sin and death? Thank God! The answer is in Jesus Christ our Lord.

Romans 7:18-25a (NLT)

TRUMP

Love trumps everything
Nothing is superior
And it never dies

Long ago the Lord said to Israel: "I have loved you, my people,
with an everlasting love. With unfailing love I have drawn you
to myself.

Jeremiah 31:3 (NLT)

Love is patient and kind. Love is not jealous or boastful or proud
or rude. It does not demand its own way. It is not irritable, and
it keeps no record of being wronged. It does not rejoice about
injustice but rejoices whenever the truth wins out. Love never
gives up, never loses faith, is always hopeful, and endures
through every circumstance. Prophecy and speaking in unknown
languages and special knowledge will become useless. But love
will last forever! Three things will last forever—faith, hope, and
love—and the greatest of these is love.

1 Corinthians 13:4-8, 13 (NLT)

CHRISTIAN HAIKU
The 17-Syllable Devotional

http://twitter.com/ChristianHaiku

www.facebook.com/pages/Christian-Haiku/ /324198840452

On the Web at:
www.christianhaiku.com

To receive daily Christian Haikus by email please send an email to
haiku@christianhaiku.com with "add me" in the subject line.